Uncertain Measures

Aidan Semmens

Uncertain Measures

Shearsman Books

First published in the United Kingdom in 2014 by
Shearsman Books
50 Westons Hill Drive
Emersons Green
BRISTOL
BS16 7DF

Shearsman Books Ltd Registered Office
30–31 St. James Place, Mangotsfield, Bristol BS16 9JB
(this address not for correspondence)

www.shearsman.com

ISBN 978-1-84861-351-5

Acknowledgements
Some of the poems in this volume have previously appeared
in the following journals. My thanks to their editors.

*Blackbox Manifold, BODY, Likestarlings, Litmus, Molly Bloom,
Notre Dame Review, Poetry Wales, Shearsman, Stride,
Tears in the Fence, 10th Muse, Under the Radar* and *The Wolf.*

CONTENTS

A Ritual Landscape	9
Beyond Imagining	16
Test Site	18
Black Light Machine	19
The Dead of the Forest	22
Dolni Ceramic	23
Terracotta Figure of a Mourning Woman	24
Amulet	25
To Dream of Falling Buildings	26
It Is Written	27
Clear the Rubble! Rebuild!	28
Walls of Troy	29
Suitable Arrangements	30
The Great North Pacific Garbage Patch	32
Against Distance	33
Gauge	35
In the Amenities Area	36
The Subversive Nature of Toys	38
An Experiment in Galvanism	40
Arizona	46
The Kiddush Cup	52
Touching Distance	54
Aldgate East	56
A Listening Station	58
The Impermanence of Rivers	62
Dust to Dust	64
Ghost Image	67
Yellow Towels	71
The Vanishing of Workers' Settlement #3	72
Fable	74
Rhapsody	76
The Remnant	79
The Jericho Tomb	81
As If	83
Test Site 2	85
Corrupt Text	87
End of the Song	90

In memory of my aunt, Lorna Arnold,
nuclear historian, 1915-2014

A Ritual Landscape

beneath the high ceilings
of the literary and scientific institute
a measurable volume of air
that would encompass the atmosphere
of several of the homes
of those who gather here
glad of the knowledge
the company or just
a cleaner lungful

the light fades in the room
as the speaker rises
high windows dimming
with evening sky
the gaslamps are lit and flare
with coalgas from the works below
listeners spit dottle and smoke
as the wisdom begins

outcropping of ore
coal iron limestone and clay
brought us here today
to work the seams
the treadles and the mills
compounding and blasting
smouldering and smelting
fresh from the waterway
the washing hangs out to dry

boats on the ouse
feel for the breeze

tugging at the wharves and staithes
the maid-of-all-work
at the works-owner's
daughter's stays
as a perfect girder
curved to exact tension
is applied to the span
transecting the river

horses work the incline
elevating and transporting
brick timber chinaclay
coke lime and forged
ingots still ticking from the foundry
barges bear away fine artefacts
axles for millwheels
tiles for the parsonage

while here on the valley side
steep where the stream carved
open the valuable strata
we institute another outlook
draw clearer breath and take
the owner and the preacher
the buyer and the banker to task

via trade line and packetboat
the traffic of desire and power
the best of all intentions
for a woman's fellow men

there are hands (damned
if not willing) waiting
to be harvested
in the forests and lakeshores
ready for putting to work
under the earth or
at the pulleys belts and wheels

molten ore blisters and glows
lighting the hillsides and sky
pours from the lip
in bright gobbets
earthen throat quenched
with fiery spirit

here the weary battleground
living water from the wooded hill
turned to fungal and mineral deposits
at the pump-mouth

what comes from the earth
to re-enter the earth
is a quantifiable volume
liths that appear to stand
freely on the surface
must be socketed securely
in stone foundations
the joints carved out with care
to a perfect lasting fit
by hands armed
with chisel axe and rasp
formed from the same hard matter

stone upon stone the blows resound
from quarryface to ritual site
the voices of men women and their children
at work on the structures
that shape their years
hard by their homes
and the fringy lake
mark-making on the land of their living

a place of gathering
an enclosure of power and spirit
sad marvels
solemnity and rejoicing
arduous paths and oblique approaches
from low hills to windblown moors

glyphs handcarved in an urban setting
diamond-hard cutting edge
of mason's craft makes
long and short work of it
mnemonic to a godfearing man
orate pro nobis

who's paid to chant
for the best rest of his soul
who takes a chance
on the mineral rights
of this man's estate

the legends are worked out
remnants left exposed to decay
under a bleak sky
dragonflies drowsily active
this late in the year

our origin myths are not set in stone
but gradually shift
in emphasis and tone from
generation to regeneration
mutating settling encrusted
with efflorescence of ore

fresh flesh
lightly undervalued
scores the structure
underlying
the tufa tougher

ultimately undone
by that capacity of flesh
for repair and regrowth

the marks in the weathering
scratches on the surface
survive a little altered
maybe but discernible to interpretation
in irretrievable eras

black box at the railhead
soft spoil and hard pipework
fossils to be read in shivered surfaces
hands soiled in toil

certain measures must be taken
samples cored and peeled
for intimate investigation
discovery and whatever may

pass up the line to the masterful
faces exposed and exhausted
exhaling lungfuls of decay
and musty air of mystery

in our fathers' ancestral dwellings
portraiture and paradox
sentiments filigreed in oxide
a ringing as on iron

low ceilings and high sacraments
bent backs and worn fingers
picking at the seams
the slow recovery of knowledge

Beyond Imagining

If the tongue were true to the voice and the voice to the thought,
How then could the world keep the lightning of the thought in
bounds? —Adam Mickiewicz

powerful winds blow over the tundra zone
eroding the ungrassed soil
a personal bonfire
of dangerous papers

infinity is not a metaphor
disaster never simply disaster
wind-borne deposits building
to sculpted structures

the future may always be terrible
the mind its own palimpsest
cannot be held to a single place
all that exists deserves to perish

modern primitive peoples make casual use
of a great variety of materials from shell
and sharks' teeth to bottle-glass
and telegraph insulators

I have the sorry desire to be happy
harnessing Jovian satellites
in the service of navigation
uncertainty as a revolutionary creed

the retreat of a glacier does not imply
backward movement of the ice itself
failure is unavoidable, what matters
is what explodes and spills, what erupts

how can you possibly believe
that a revolution can or should be mastered
or known in advance
if you are in touch with those

parts of the mind which the mind
itself cannot master
freedom is always the freedom
to think otherwise

dark spots creep continuously
across the surface of the sun
the past an artefact
blank time before ones birth

with the return of warm climate the river revives
enough to resume erosion in the normal way
this method of time-measurement has not
yet been widely applied but it promises much

a perilous path between heaven revered
and heavens revealed
through a telescope unravelling
as a challenge to human intelligence

people of the insulator culture
seek ways to monetise their artefacts
the middle finger of Galileo's right hand
encased in a gilded glass egg

Test Site

what I may tell you about
is the morning they tested Galileo
on a 500-foot tower
before doomed Joshua trees

the horizon in turmoil
giving no idea of the scale
the brilliance of the flash
that fuses sand into glass

a sharp and slightly painful click
precedes the thunder
a hollow sphere the size and weight of a bowling-ball
a cobra about to strike

much that has happened
cannot be talked about for years
soldiers hammering on the door
framed in a leaky authority

a condition of perpetual emergency
the fires of Hiroshima were mostly caused
by kerosene cookers preparing breakfast
knocked over by the percussion wave

model railway associations and private
societies for propagating mushroom lore
are enemies of the state and the Bureau
for Supervision of Production Aesthetics

Black Light Machine

from a distance it looks like
a giant cuneiform text
a series of metal frames and panels
many of the filters lipstick-stained

cadmium red streams weaving
across a territory drawn
with yellow rectangles and
abstract forms

shiny pipelines winding
through a forest
arbitrary lines propped
up by mythology

heaped high in rundown
wooden houses near city walls
revellers and merchants
fat as clay icons

reeking of perfume
wigs and false eyelashes
lost in the void of prevention
and avoidable passion

up tiny filthy narrow stairs
airless beds with stained sheets
brave words and a decadent
preoccupation

your gaze strays over
tangled ribbons of the intersection

uranium run-off coating the ground
with a white residue

a blue tractor in a diagonal field
lichen patterns on forgotten hoardings
apparatus of tubes
rails and roadways looping

representations of tidal flux
a sophisticated system
of refrigeration
treatments that work in minutes

in a landscape of logistics sheds
and information hubs
construction of national borders
kissing the dust-caked cars

white vinyl to protect the paintwork
with a clashing set of symmetries
broken hulls of ships
in a sea of unused tyres

the monstrousness of facelifts
and preposterous tombs
incredible among holy images
piled in alcoves and doorways

a mausoleum of old toothbrushes
assemblage of cooling units
a vast teeming trading floor
tobacco growers at the mercy of infidels

anthropology of lost gestures
replicas purchased among crowds

the only choice possible
between heresy and unbelief

between mud and bathos
we transgress the way the road lies
a marbled pattern on the water's surface
meaning justifying the end

The Dead of the Forest

the vanishing point where the lines converge
recedes at a steady rate, staying
always the same distance
in the unmeasurable past

in the enclosing dark
capturing the space we move through
you can't see the trees for the wood
but occasionally a bird

flies from one side to the other
unknown—you catch
the flash of its wing
even a snatch of song

above the unchanging rhythm and rattle
of wheels on jointed track, and there
in the corner of your eye
is after all an irregular feature in the gloom

an uneven wall of lichened concrete
half grown-over, a patch
of disturbing earth where
nothing now happens

Dolni Ceramic

wifely wisdom
the carpenter's song
and the sculptor's
surreptitious ceremony
a little whittling
a quiet caress of clay
by the carefully aligned hearth
long nights of winter

transgressional text
imparted before the fact
or supposition of inscription
where wife intends
no more or less than woman
with no male inferred
except in the pregnant truth
her breasts pendulous
tendentious
umbilical oval incised
eyes mere slits
at crazy angles
alien life force
driven against tundra snow
and the drift of her hips

Terracotta Figure of a Mourning Woman

not mourning merely
but wailing
face contorted by grief
and the sculptor's thumb

a cry of loss perceived
in soft lines
of hard clay preserved
for millennia

the mourner
herself lost
as the maker
and their language

children and lovers
entitlement and pain
great things
and blasphemies

all the certainties of a life
unstitched its structure shredded
a family committed to quicklime
or force of fire

skulls grown unknowingly
under vanished skin
turned to artefact
surface as friable to the fingers

Amulet

to watch the skin grow slowly over the wound
to hear the twisting metal
to sense the sun abandoning the field
to shady winter

mellifluous dissonance of strange instruments
fractures in the snowsheet
rumble of passage on perilous roads
in beckoning distance

to fear the pain of eruption in the flesh
to taste the fading ember
to feel the fire exhibiting its strength
of unknown purpose

figurines of fortune assumed
to invest dignity and power in the grave
a thing of strange beauty and perfection
carved from the thighbone of a slave

To Dream of Falling Buildings

the dust billows out in a doughnut ring
surprisingly quickly round the lower floors
a roughly even distance from the walls
then hangs suspended in the air
as if holding the waves of sound

below the bridge a shattered silver reliquary
remains in silt partly composed
of particles of ink and paper
combined in intricate designs of law and rite
once carefully prescribed

corpses under the brilliantined water
will reveal themselves only when putrefaction
has bloated them and they rise
to break the surface
with stretched and polished hides

there is a face in the shivered reflection
by the bank where a wall once stood
or maybe it's a trick of the light
and there is no reality
beyond what is possible to know

It Is Written

the document is redacted
which does not reveal but conceals
the identities of those presumed guilty

a borrowed language shifts
seasons migrate

repentance and revenge
slow feasting and erudition
make strange bedfellows

a hand on a handle
a cuffed wrist pushing
at an open door

beyond the sound of laughter
and a glimpse of children
partaking of games
from which their mothers
have been excluded

in an autonomous region
the sky clouds over or
the burnished sun bursts through
just as we reach the unscaleable wall
on which it is written
this wall will fall

Clear the Rubble! Rebuild!

because for the moment there is no cinema
a golden opportunity is before us—
clearing the ruins won't do it
it's not pleasurable enough
we must find the language
to reach people who are working hard

the industrialist with his briefcase extends a hand
to the glowing smile of the countryman
cradling a sheaf of corn
on the ministry's ceramic façade
the power lines whisped
into perspectival distance

the urban human sunbathes on the balcony
of his light modern airy apartment
leads a sober existence
a few sad love affairs and a life
spent rehearsing those little adulteries
of its youth

we must have music and entertainment
yet form without content means nothing
a poet who co-operates may be allowed
some difficult figures of speech
the urban human lies on a practical sofa
and does not use the bathtub for his animals

Walls of Troy

from that excessive salient
if you could climb so high
you'd see the ships the sails the sea
the sun glinting on windows in the west

long-buried hints of
secret concordats betrayed
a lake steaming in the morning sun
ominous with hazardous potential

a steel structure studded
with concrete and glass
shards at implausible angles like
soles of shoes torn off in the desert

a tarry scarred place
of oilcan homesteads
jewelled swordhilts and aerosols
tankers rusting in the breakers

where heroes' corpuscles mingle into silicon
particles with a whiff of pesticide
and a stain upon their garments
flapping in the scrubby wind

Suitable Arrangements

the vehicles stop at a bend in the road
a painting of ancient domesticity
where the travellers get some food
a squat terracotta teapot with tiny cups
a dish of river fish, scrambled eggwhites
tiny dusty birds sing in cages
hung from the branches of trees
we have become accustomed to the houses
spilling over the desert hillsides
people drink tea and commit adultery
faces inclining to the warmth of the sun
children play with their reflections in the mirror
washing spread over hedges to dry

one of the men steps outside to see what's happening
the building is an outpost against the dark
a life all about its childhood
isolated exotic acts of violence
in time we get better at asking questions
place excessive trust in the image
the lights are not defeated by the desert
a series of tiny films in vulnerable terrain
it would be hard not to feel
a pang of regret at wreckage made neat
by the cleansing force of the sea
a wall of black water vast and incongruous
exquisitely wrapped boxes, a few
brightly illuminated vending machines
white china dishes unbroken and unclaimed
radiation measured in food and breast milk

on both banks of the river
are shrines and sculptures, cabbages
growing where a bedroom was
it is almost night or almost morning
huge bonfires are lit on the beaches
for the ghosts to find their way to shore
the machinery of knowledge connects
territories to the metropole, arrangements
must be made for the children

The Great North Pacific Garbage Patch

stirred by the gyre, swept
by mesoscale eddies,
the particles of plastic mesh
and play, somewhere between
volcanic swirl and the confusion
of small children in a ball pool

elements of faded colour
and language intermixed,
instructions for unpackaging,
assembly and hazard warnings
in polyglot mélange,
Chinese, German and bad English

circuits diagrammed in the currents
of air and water syntactically applied
to the killer potential of
drift-net balls and polythene snares
washing towards wild shores
of multi-coloured plastic sands

Against Distance

a long journey by rail from the place
a man may lie dying
we hold hands in the dark
bright healthy children play round the fence

the eyes are ambiguous
whether those of woman or man
young person or old
even perhaps those of a child

contented or pleading
where torture may be involved
I am not sure I want to know
the sun rising above the summits

of autumn-stricken trees
bleeds into the room
the light a blessing and an invasion
through the frame of the doorway

we view a wide landscape
in which the hero silhouetted
against distance
may be approaching or leaving

gross colour an imposition on sense
a trick of the light
in awe then alarm
the most alarming space

space disappearing
an isolated disc of stone and brick

days of esoteric contemplation
with incredible letters from far-off tides

Gauge

calibrated to a fine degree of artistry
your antique chronometer
ticks off the nice limits
to what we know

outside the temple
under a gentle snow
a broken altimeter lies
silently rusting
temperature's fall unnoted

with what sophistication do we measure
moral rectitude of the Inuit
buying bullets at the supermarket
to dispatch with hand-tooled rigour

and long-honed precision to a point
the right brief distance behind the eye
of a blubber-rich seal-calf
out there on the blue expanse of ice

foot down inches above the tarmac
in the cab of a ravening vehicle
eating up the kilometres
mile after mile washed down
with copious servings of arctic oil

on a post by the roadside a crow
closely watches a buzzard watching
the verge intent on snatching
a morsel of its next kill

In the Amenities Area

arcane projection from the sepulchre
sweet day of eradicable pain

railway ribbons stretch, bulking
monstrous rivets into the green
earth, claiming territory
for the kind of people who own
other people, their sweat

and those parts of skin exude
passion and compassion
to soluble form: a generation
ago all this was virgin
and will revert in time
to something like

fresh wax, an impression
passion for the possible
bespoke tailoring
stains on a cuff

your impossible voice
caressing the blue
sky, white clouds

scudding for miles in a single
light puff, shadowing
glacial scars become populated

with TV aerials and outdoor netties

scraps of newsprint telling
six impossible stories before
industrial bacon and stolen eggs
ketchup stains on porcelain

music and mathematics
mirrorballs and monsters
the mythy magic of an African deathmask
brave faces and fractured bones
church steeple erupting from a froth of green
fields where workers toil, grim visages poised
over trout streams, alert for a kill

dazzled by dappled evening sun
the driver failed to see the warning light
his truck sprawls in the ditch
cargo of live pigs some crushed and squealing
while others roam the fields of wheat and beet

Methodism and magic
mercury and mills
intemperate rising of steam and green corn
paths of righteousness cut through hillside woods
where indentured boys run wild after work
conkers fought and beechnuts chewed
the sly taste of blood on a lichened knuckle

corporate knives are out
for paring unnecessary flesh
from the carcase
of a small family firm
in these uncertain times

this sucker could go down

The Subversive Nature of Toys

the future carries with it the archaic
a faint glimpse of light from a faraway galaxy
the intrinsic energy of empty space
what is important is the mean of the data

variable equation-of-state quintessence
the fascination that issues from the flayer's zone
sweet sticky odour of putrefaction
the corpse so palpable in its morbidity

I dug a lake and planted trees
curves fitting to the theory of errors
a dusty place where even priests and kings
lie in darkness, clad

like birds in coats of feathers
blasphemers hang by their tongues
adulterers by their genitals
eternity as a state of constant nostalgia

punishment of the wicked is a reversal
of the natural order, the actual
or accurate value
of a physical quality

such as length, time interval
or temperature cannot be found—
measuring devices
may be faulty in various ways

the dead watch us, a democracy of ghosts
the unclasped spirit of Patroclus

like a vapour gone beneath the earth
gibbering faintly

such errors follow no simple law
and in general arise from many causes
nothing immaterial has freed itself
from mysterious connection to the meat

heaven's existence is dependent on its impossibility
god laughs at the punishment of sinners, predestined
condemned by his own will and the lack of theirs
an ordinary sin-set, forgivable fallibilities

the damned writhing below in chaotic torture
their great numbers confining the victims
in unbearable stench of flames that give no light
cataclysmic explosions from self-destructive stars

I ferried him who had no boat
no measures of dispersion
systematic errors may arise
from the observer or the instrument

death and its rituals of decay
are noises off, the only worth
to be assigned to the corpse
its break-up value

the calculus of risk, a pragmatic
assessment of interest
the mean frequency
is usually not of particular significance

An Experiment in Galvanism

I: MAY 16, 1791 *

in veil of tears
to whose fault
do you ascribe
the drowned vault

Alessandro Volta throws the switch
that illuminates a venerable text
hand-coloured, light-flooded
interconstellationary wave
tingles on the tongue

of which we speak
through fantastical device
dependent chaotically
on quasi-divine algorithm
of a suppurating sun

the natural philosopher engages matter
in terms to give us pause
force fissure in the zeitgeist

saints are sculpted boys
below the waterline
efflorescence of recovered paint
in borrowed time
mementi mori, moisture
forcing up the floor

we count the bedes
right-lateral side-slip
compressional forces
expressed as uplift

*day of the most severe quake yet to strike Connecticut;
in Pisa, Volta commences experiments with Galvanism.*

II: RE ACTION
IN FORMATION

a lifeforce flows in these magnetic patterns
fielding an iron planet, filling joyful
beings with premonitions of disasters;
electric impulses compel our muscles
to acts of faith or defiance; video
conferences take place behind these shut

doors; the rhythmic valves open and shut
in isometric, biographic patterns
reduced to blip and pulse in video-
graphic representation of every joyful,
wilful or unwitting move of muscles;
our best intention may lead to disasters

piled in smoky pile upon disasters
in dusty cities; rivermouths are shut
by seismic spasm of tectonic muscles
contracting in hyperperistaltic patterns;
musical forms ignite a simple joyful
neurotransmitted response on video

screens in quiet chambers; video
games erupt in choreographed disasters
from flights of finger four formation, joyful
pilots in lockdown, quiescent suspects shut
in soundproofed rooms; psychodramatic patterns
provoke involuntary moves in muscles

sensitised to allegory, muscles
attuned to catastrophic video

representation of ideas in patterns
that predicate predicted grave disasters;
we enter this with all our senses shut,
minds in denial, heartbeat oddly joyful,

the tip of each finger four points to turn joyful,
exciting contradictions in the muscles;
the strongest light, whether eyes open or shut,
four minutes, our pictures and home video—
there's never any shortage of disasters
laid on each other in interwoven patterns

our valves tight shut, our altimeter joyful
with flexing patterns of our complex muscles
reduced to video, seconds from disasters

III: THE AGE OF INSECURITY

it takes an expense of will
(or an effort of wing)
to reach this point
from where we look down on
milling humanity, a city
quietly pulsing (as if
a living city ever achieves quiet)
taking the path of least
resistance between hillocks
as it spreads to overwhelm

the rising smoke, biblically
miraculous, conventionally claims
the epithet 'plume' as if
a feather could ever
be this threatening, yet

we see, in our uniquely
privileged moment, how this
metaphor might also apply
to an escape of oil
in deep sea, ink on a quill
written into the terrifying world
where the innocent eye sees nothing

no pattern in the shape the rocks take
or the inbuilt obsolescence of highrise
blocks that will flex with the mantle
only so far, strain maps of bridges
with colossal catapult potential

should they lose their bearings
in the good earth

blurring the continuities
we take one element for another,
water for breathing, plutonium for fire,
catastrophism as a way of life

in the 17th century some scientists
wanted shot of Aristotle,
the Swift response ridicule
of the scientists (a category
not yet so defined)

Edison was no scientist but an entrepreneur,
the electric chair an advertising gambit;
dams at Niagara might have powered Atlantic City,
current turning one wheel to spin another
as a photovoltaic sun
lights up the Vegas night

and what of Volta now?
his name subsumed, an eddy in the currents
swirled with Ampere and Watt

the pattern's in the pile,
affairs cunningly woven and
trodden underfoot

Arizona

for Sandy Kunzer

Tombstone to Monument
the evilhearted Chevy bucks
rebellious under his boot on the gas
saguaro sunset silhouetted

pretty purple posies a carpet of green
in a brown landscape a vine
that does not harm the tree it climbs
human additives crowding out natives

the mint is horehound flavouring candy
taking over the septic leach field
love grasses, bullfrogs, mesquites
crawfish, salt cedar and homo sapiens

the soft glow of luminaries
light the mission interior, white flowers
of the sacred datura bloom
grave markers of a disused cabin

oaks of Cochise Stronghold
women grind acorns and seed into meal
in bedrock mortars of granitic
Council Rocks

> *Hercules Spectre Spooky II*
> *Phantom Stratolifter Skyhawk*
> *Raven Orion B-52*
> *Stratotanker Stratofortress Aardvaark*

Dauntless Scorpion Viking Sioux
Delta-Dagger Freedom-Fighter Tomcat
Sabre Cargomaster Caribou
Chickasaw Chocktaw Seabat

a diversity of rock types, structures
and topography, processes of continental collision
and separation, erosion and deposition
the oldest rocks belong to a mappable formation

pinal schist, deep sea sediments, volcanic ejecta
metamorphosed beyond genesis, plutonic igneous
rocks on the east side of the Whetstone
and Huachuca mountains

sandstones formed in deserts or on beaches
limestones in shallow seas, shales
deposited as clay in ancient marshes or mudflats
conglomerates formed in alluvial fans

as at Ash, Stump and Miller canyons
as debris continues to fill the valleys
rivers form with power to cut into the fill
the same water eroding the surface at work beneath

rainwater percolating into the ground
has created the wet, living cave
sculpting inorganic crystalline solids
tuff shearing roughly at the western edge

Rockwell-Lancer Globemaster III
Starlifter Starfire Silver-Star
Tigercat Bearcat Tracker Banshee
Seahorse Peacemaker Seastar

Albatross Samaritan Tigershark
F-111 Fighting-Falcon
Tigereye Tiger II Pavehawk
Sabre-Dog Panther Demon

goldeneye blooms in a grassy meadow
pyrrhuloxia on the trumpetvine
red beak a badge
in service for camouflage

chickenroll, catfish and banoffee pie
ice-cream in 17 confections, deep
pink jelly of the prickly
pear, beer at gas-station prices

Mexico, Korea and east Europe
meet in the desert
where food is piled
high and wages low

what do central Americans dream
of dust on the interstate
coyotes scavenging roadkill
by a semi bound for Yuma

dry air of the high plain
keeps old craft fresh
for sudden shock
in some hereafter

outside the mission children climb
a rocky mound to a white-
washed cross, claimant
of land for an alien faith

walking on rustless wings
in a no-fly zone
elegant trogon, red plumage barred
by an aerial shadow in harsh light

Starfighter Thunderchief Compass-Call
Shooting-Star Trojan Ranger
Black-Spot Buckeye Clipper
Thunderstreak Thunderflash Cougar

Tracer Trader Neptune Provider
Skyraider Skywarrior Sentry
Spooky Hornet Night-Intruder
Thunderjet Vigilante

walk, don't walk, the sidewalk
bleeds into scrubland
Rita Ranch, suburbia
cattlefencing the wild

fighters and bombers
ranked behind wire mesh
hens in the desert fox's coop
fast going nowhere

in the fastnesses
of time and the desert
bare bones unfleshed
by saguaro's slow death

endless arrowing haulage
viewed from ribbon height
startling peaks in the mirror
objects nearer than they appear

anhydrous atmosphere
of the high caves
preserves dung millennia
after the sloth's extinction

fresher than yesterday
the golfcourse green
or the tempting neck
of the shaded defile

here in clear air
we watch the skies, listen
for pulses, beats and echoes
a rattler's warning

> *Northrop-Spirit Nightingale*
> *Galaxy Extender Mercury*
> *Blackbird Voodoo Crusader*
> *Stratojet Hustler Fury*

caryatid and katydid
among stones
alien beauty
of an unsoiled land

fragile chaos
between crystal and grit
synaptic fluids
in a semi-rigid stem

this supposed desert
is alive with possibilities
cheap metamorphosis
of systemic fluff

it's the living end
demands investigation
at a sub-atomic level
the little evolutions are inescapable

in Sonoran sunrise grey
fades to orange to blue
coyote calls become memory
the horizon indistinct

The Kiddush Cup

the wine is not red but pale amber
no blood is drunk even symbolically
the drops make no lasting stain
as the cup overflows with blessings

ten gouts dipped from the glass
while another grand chalice stands
awaiting any possible entrance
by the anticipated harbinger

in linen boots at the vintage season
the grapes are trodden
to separate the good
from the impure

at each drink of four one takes
more than half a cup
each containing liquid
equal to one and a half eggs

the goblets incorporate saucers
to catch the spill in which
the braided ceremonial candles
must be extinguished

before the people were taken away
the vineyards reached to the hilltop
where now the thicket and woods
have reclaimed the earth

on a muddy island in the river
fringed by a tangle of reeds
a tribe of stones moulders
inscriptions become indecipherable

Touching Distance

fragmented light chimes
on broken edges
shivered shards that hurt
the back of the eye

unslip the mask gently
damage what is unseen
the ritual blade
of a hand a ferryboat

smoking its way
across a channel
glinting
in slanting rain

the moon a scimitar
Venus appended
signet and sickle
structure

ominous Mars
may be a satellite
blinking or your blood
pounding

pent energy and pictograms
darkening skies
red with rust
a dream of evasion

boldly and stealthily
by way and stream steering

by landmark
familiar and unknown

wood and stone
a place of gathering
here and then
mark-making

on the land
of our living
sad marvels
across low hills

arduous pathways
trajectories untaken
in the dark
earth and fitted stone

the cool of cut surfaces
smell of soil and bodies
standing water
and flowing

a hand on an arm
a breath of your breath
lightly
touching

Aldgate East

The only good life is one in which there is no need for miracles
—*Nadezhda Mandelstam*

there is a tree, a railing and then the corpse
of a bicycle, beyond it a shining tower
where executives come and go
lights reflecting in their shoes
as they ignore the place where stony earth
has broken through the paving

we may not believe in Greek gods
but everywhere see their powers at work
the possibility of extreme revelation
in an abandoned coach station
standing water full of broken
instruments and scraps of paper

there are pockets of ancient superstition
around the entrances to the underground
railway, signs of an outlived revolution
glimpsed in the windows of the public bar
a moment of subtle and absolute transition
between the needle and the traffic

to believe in something blatantly untrue
it is necessary to interrogate
the history of certainty and doubt
cigarette packs of a half-forgotten brand
and the memory of a flavour that subsists
only in boxes of unwritten postcards

diaries scribbled in indelible pencil
pale and silvery between discolorations
patches of decayed meaning
among the ambiguous machinery
discarded, perilously tilted
over greening rubble slopes

to live in this resculpted place
awaiting the changing lights
deception becomes second nature
relics concealed in a marble block
the woman as she crosses the street
has no name in the film of her life

A Listening Station

you now enter
the not-for-profit sector
cannot contain good news
for the Turks and North Africa
compete to sell me
"the Red Army" hats and signs
hot dog stands by
Chinese restaurant or
occupies part of the site
intended to inspire awe once
for a millennium
pieces that vain
date debris
building project
unearthed by workers
digging to replace Soviet block
for housing component of the privileged
with shiny office
of multinational banks

memorial to fallen leaves or
jump and swing among teenagers and
mothers with strollers converse
the phones lit
with elegantly suited apparatchiks
enterprise museum
souvenir stand
multimedia presentation (with
interactive touchscreen symbolism
added and fries) or

US corporation that flag
flies through it all
illuminated by reflected glow of the spotlight
gracefully from the setting sun

the heart is a mountain road
in east-west direction running
unfinished and already secured
with a fence
the devil hills'
walls equipped with ears

the ministry did not confirm or deny
or she holds any information within
mountain gravel cover
the unfinished building of the university
of a defence that has nothing but a number
but some demolition was
already some foundations and pattern
from the attic to the end of work

amorphous materials from room 75/038
a mass of paper yarn and black fleck
telephone conversation among the party elite
comprehension of high priority
a motor mechanic with a list of employees and why
they might be enticed insight
into weakness exploited

immured incinerator liftshaft and shredders
self-domestic facilities for staff
including wood-panelled courtyard lined
intelligence personnel and linguists
drill a hole in the floor a dark interior

·

all samples a high fibre count
structural black fleck could be remnants
of carbon paper: where do these
documents now? high
mineral content of the material and
frequency of entomological
violation of the site reflect low pollen
and plant material evidence
the lack of windows

on each bus or U-Bahn
women hold property eye
in context of busy crowded
hustle and bustle and jostle it
on the tray of cake
in plastic fragile shell

the night S-Bahn
man is too fat to be contained
in one place part one of the thighs and seat
and unleashed trainer/coach rendering the
opposite unoccupiable
lolls snoring ears plugged
with Sony products
and probably misses his stop

excavators were far below
fugitives who crave jeans and Marlboro
those obedient staff
mining data
whose whereabouts and progress
day-by-day calm loyalty
and possible death have been reported
for those whose movements are directed

secretly intercept
because a man which Blake by name
incorrectly credited ideology
is pressured into private life
or enjoys to play spy

in river while digging piles
for the new
construction and excavator grab
every silver object of devotion and ritual
cast on the waters
by the "minions of history"
battered and blackened on
night of pogrom and infamous
for those few recusants
who else might put faith
in doctrines gone to the wall
should be a daily bile flavour
in advertising at bus stops wrily
Toys'R Us on Karl-Marx Straße

The Impermanence of Rivers

Hannah daughter of my neighbour
is handicapped by terror of beautiful things
the blade which cuts a swathe across the heath
the old machinery rusting in the heather

uncertainty is what the heathen has
that tolerance of men and strangers
the inadequacy of love
hatred and rage conflated confused

rain accumulating on moortops
percolates through peat to trickle
unseen though sometimes heard
via reens and gulleys

pipe and culvert
to ditch brook stream and runnel
watermeadow lake and fen
estuary tidal flats to the sea

an angler shelters by nylon windbreak
set up against the offshore blow
on a beach of cobble stones
line taut to the bold grey wave

cranes crash and grind
boats bob winter wheels
in muted splendour of the sky
which constrains all

from up here the water is a curling
scar slashed across the land
skylight gleaming
on roads of escape

Hannah is hampered by the fear of beauty
the erosive power of wind and water
flints worn round and gentle by the sea
the blade which cuts a path against the tide

Dust to Dust

and to your left
the uncertainties of Ariadne
ponderous vertical
markers over
sunswept territory
the air has a splintery resonance all its own

pollutant quotient of the breath we draw
pelt peeled back in labs and civic streets
in fettered rage
on a fetid tide

the air is almost solid
you may walk through it
only with difficulty

fragmented light chimes
on the broken edges
shivered shards that hurt
the back of the eye

a light dust lies
on all we touch
your hand on my arm
the speaking wound
carved out offence

a foggy mountain buries its dead in plunge pools
innocence washed away
with fragments of lichen and moss

small eddies of bubbles
white on the surface
carcinoma flecks
on clotted skin

through the half-open window at night
listen for such borrowings
as train whistles coyote calls
wind in castle walls

hear the willows tugging
tying down in blown cascades
the unseen crimson
of erotic pain—

a half-healed cut
torn open on a snag in the bedding
an envisioned stain
in the dark by the bookcase
a picturehook hanging
without a picture

in the necropolis
countless small artefacts
of undetermined age and use:
the broken steering-column
of a 1968 Ford
a double-edged knife
intricately worked blade
cut and shut
practised as an intimate deception
under the fingernails
traces of blood
roughly sloughed skin

minutely growing crack in the stone
evidences seismic life below
scorn of Poseidon
in a fallout shelter

web of deceit
party flavours
hard to swallow

mesh of rumblings
Judith with the head of Holofernes
intractable entrails dangling

palace of gods on a white hillside
broken down
by time
and faltered belief

fissile plutonium has a half-life
of a thousand human generations

Ghost Image

musically barely literate, nevertheless
I hear the fiddle and my heart dances
tattoos on the shiny kitchen floor
as, sharp blade in hand, I move
to the implicit beat and the board
where the fresh meat oozes by the stove
awaiting
        (in its chemical bath
        the prepared paper lies soaking)
the fiddle is no
violin but the simulacrum
of its playing engineered to stimulate
the waves in this room in my time
the time I beat
with the knife
in my hand
upon disanimated flesh
lightly raising
the volume
the tempo
and the heat
olfaction joined to syncopation

of strange heritance, the knife
bears Hitler's emblem
on the haft
the blade
diminished by oxidation
to a less acute edge
threatening a dirtier cut
        (in the liquid
        colouration suggests image)

the passage of the implement
from haematite and other ores
to my grandmother's drawer
casts many questions
concerning manufacture
of metal and motive
of chemical and social structures
of lives on brown stairwells
the smell of aircraft oils
leather aprons
thin paper in dusty rooms
the processes and aftermath
of cookery

days like these we think of as brown
might equally be blue or grey
barelimbed trees and featureless sky oppress
just a little, calmly, obliquely
as if a Tuesday of no intent
the colours bleeding
without meaning
    (the image intensifies, solidifies
     in what may be faces)
in secret passages between houses
we pass soundlessly
as seamlessly
as we are able
our ghosts going before us
we are no more
than what we think we remember
of who we may think we might be
though the walls seemed solid enough

before the bombs
and the year-by-year depredations
of seepage, slippage
and invasive creeping plantlife

flesh carved away, corpuscles
indifferent to the pain
that is not mine or yours
blade embedded to the hilt
the handle becomes hard
to work, to shank
the muscle from the bone
      (the shades and their shadows
      darken to an intensity of sepia)
an unkindness that pares
the necessary and unnecessary
together, syncopated
to another desire or whim
feel the point and edge
investigate the interstices
of fibre and fibre, slyly separate
membrane from cell, memory
from predicted outcome
the music swelling
in another key
a tonal shift of precision
a poisonous ambience

the knife with the swastika handle
is no longer with us
its passing unlikely but never remarked
you were anyway never quite
comfortable with it
its stained steel curiously
light and misbalanced in your fingers

(the faces and stances
　　seem dimly recalled—
a wedding scene in a fakely silvered frame
ivy-covered walls and shaded windows
with the hint of an observer
peering from behind the glass
at the assembled party
a dog in a bow-tie
pleased among its people
uncle George ironic, a little to one side
pipe in hand removed from his mouth for the picture
later to die
a sailor's death
or some other
among the box of papers on the shelf

Yellow Towels

for Catherine Hales

but India does have an odour?
can Germany? yet it is the sense
reminiscent scent that brings me
in the sense of India
German bathroom in mind
not today but 30 years ago
India as a newer state (and this
room totally in other state)
and perhaps it is only coincidence
the soap that you wash your towels
oil and incense or mosquito spray
in another house I used to stay
perhaps the lingering fragrance of a garland
hung around the sepia portrait hint
I cannot fill in missing loved relative
the densely packed fading blooms
matching your towels in a yellow tint

The Vanishing of Workers' Settlement #3

down a winding path
in a shadowy scene
a woman and a man are pushing
a wagon loaded with industrial implements

you must guess at their concerns
which if any of the huddled huts
in the barely focused background
may be their homestead

or their place of work
whether the dog standing alone
in what might pass for a village street
is theirs or maybe a wolf

heavy with traditional symbolism
strayed from the vestigial forest
that crowds at the edges
vignetting the pastoral view

down winding paths the people
and the powerful fragment
a strategic actor looks for ways
to achieve goals of hegemony

the magnetic energy of acts of exchange
in the field of ideas and perception
under powerlines the elements of coercion
in that perpetual plebiscite of desires

the leaking of confidential documents
is carefully aimed ferocious and destructive

with few and precise preliminaries
disunity is easy to achieve

in ankle-deep snow through which
you might glimpse rails
a huddle of the elderly pushes a cart
that brings the weekly delivery

the village itself barely more
than a row of wooden sheds
or barracks interspersed sparsely
with small garden plots

things have been falling apart
since the onset of modernity
fragmentation as the condition of knowledge
the extortion of desire extraction of obedience

from Petersburg to Trieste a different
model of the family pertains
clusters of matryoshki
in posters on the metro

many of the buildings
have collapsed into themselves
or been taken over by goats
and stray dogs treading eerie pathways

even against reprehensible authority
protest may shade into malice
revolt into viciousness levels of fertility
began to decline even before the revolution

Fable

first snows of the year
and a skater's track on the ice

bitten fingers reaching
for a familiar scuffed volume

monochrome image of outdated fashions
a postcard on a dusty shelf

a book is an overgrown cemetery
where the names must be guessed

ashes of a dead tree
that still holds its living shape

weapons heaped in anterooms
while a town emits its smoke

nothing much here moves
that is vigorous or unbloodied

the sound is of distantly cracking beams
and of beetles emerging from holes in the walls

you yearn to walk on wild shores
sifting multi-coloured sand through your fingers

the ebb and flow of glacial tides
scouring new topographies

globalisation of birds
migrating across continents

the attendant at your ceremony
dances on the head of a pin

do not be seduced by the illusion of peace

Rhapsody

how can I kiss your dust?
I am your dust
for every new song
you can find an old tune
almost never does a diary contain
literary experiments
of a technical or stylistic nature
like a photograph it accrues
the weight and authority
of reality itself
neither wisdom nor prayer will help
when the harvest fails
there will possibly come a time
when these words are published

we find ourselves in an alien place
among the smell of things
we are not used to seeing
the passage of time calculated
by the possibility of food
autonomy is fictitious
every evening our shoes
are confiscated
but with weeping you pay no debts
neither with cursing nor with laughter
can the world be remade
the element of optimism is present
in the view of the factory chimney
which as long as it smokes
gives promise of continued existence

all I have lived through until this moment
was normality
part of a world
in which one continued
to be a human being
we had nothing
yet lacked for nothing
all I should like to have in life
at the present moment
is plenty to eat
neither wisdom nor prayer

there is little sure knowledge
of what is happening
and opinions vary—
who are any of us
after all? a man
is only human
and sometimes not even that

I will eat the carrots
as I harvest them and never
go far from my garden
this is not the moment for adventure
these abandoned courtyards
a symbol of danger
not of freedom
the next goal
is to defeat the winter
I shall cook potatoes and millet
which I have never eaten before
today in school I managed to win
a third soup while outside
someone was burning
and I saw the men look away

we have many sicknesses but amnesia
is not one of them
we have been left with nothing
but the letters of our alphabet
just exactly how things are
is impossible to imagine
those who have not been witness
will never comprehend these events
those who have never able
to reveal them fully

how can I kiss your dust?
I am your dust
for every new tune
there is an old song

the desire to write is strong
as the repugnance of words
we want to believe
there is some sense in still being
but it is an obligation
to remember the past in the future
with neither cursing nor laughing the handing-on
indispensable take note of this document
for it contains important material

The Remnant

in public rooms
the men are dancing
the women waiting

a bell rings out
or it may be a shot
crack of a whip or glass

no one hears
or affects not to hear

it is winter
and no one knows
if it will ever be spring

hooded at the wire
the kneeling man
takes upon him
no one's sins but those

of his accusers
curses, denies, forgives
or cannot forgive

a thousand curtains, scrolls
silver and brass, fine embroidery
disconnected mute fragments
stacked up as if for sale

the orphaned books
held in your hands
grimy with their smell

a city known
for its chemical works
and leather goods

profiles of roofless shells
on a wide cobbled street
with loading platforms

scraping at hints
of what may have been
we find scraps of evidence
of what is forgotten
or was meant to be

it would once have been unimaginable
what we are trying to know

the men go on dancing
the women waiting

The Jericho Tomb

all flesh gone
the skeletons preserved
(few bones
damaged or missing)
by dry desert air
and mine-deep isolation
for resurrection
beyond kingdoms and empires
behind glass
in which the flashes
of a thousand cameraphones
reflect and glare

today everyone is exulting
but who can tell
what the future will bring
where you meet your tower of Babel
languages and ritual uprooted
from their lands and gathered
in hope of liberation

the learned one says we must cry
for the living and the dead
the wise says rejoice
for hard times are coming

this is where our aspiration
was born and grew
though we felt like beggars
in this wilderness

of a thousand huts
and wandering dogs
where all that moves now
is the sand

As If

What is it really? As if we possessed the understanding to
know what 'really' is   —Tom Keve, Triad

reverential garments
folded carefully
in a dark wooden drawer

a candle burning in an empty room
where soon for lack of oxygen
it may sputter and fail

a painted feather in an open field
print on the pages
of an old and heavy book

all the meanings you can put a name to
assembled under cover of nearing dawn
a thought experiment

of shameful origin
presenting the manifest image
of a god that absented itself

to create nothing
the void essential
for emergence of a phenomenal universe

the appearance of matter
a partial glow
rudiments of belief

and chemistry
reality is a psychic phenomenon
the observer its co-creator

the act of measurement decides
what is to be measured
and must result in uncertainty

the electron is a wave
the electron is a particle
why must we glorify the lack of contradiction?

Test Site 2

we knew where to look
because of the searchlights
in the great band of desert
I can barely see the torch
through the dark welding glasses
as we waited for the fried
chicken and lemonade and chocolate
some crazy optimist in suntan oil
like Galileo donning
opinion without evidence
for his audience with the pope

I behind the windscreen
weapons carrier
the silver flash of white
patch of purple
still going strong when I closed my eyes
like Galileo's negative gravity
under the torch
power of persuasion

and I turned back to look
on the land of white
sky irradiated with yellow light
darkening to orange gradually
reveals the white of new cloud
fireball begins to rise
fade and flicker
stir the fire swirling churning
three miles wide
the stem the strain of the smoke

swirling smoke
glows in purple
majestic rise
from the smoke and dust
and loud crack sharp end
roaring thunder following
soundtrack a minute 40 seconds late
Galileo counting off the time
under report of the tower
the log falling

it is a beautiful sight from the air
glass glaze green sand melted
a mile-wide lens
cratered in the centre
in the desert of brown

Corrupt Text

For any truth to exist one must be able to make a false claim about it

all along the tracks
we saw the soldiers
and the war machines

a system of complicated traps
and the way the light scores your pathway
making the footing precarious

a statue of Lenin brought down to size
so you can see the pitting in the granite skull
run your hand over the lichened brow

pockets of ancient superstition
in the indistinct and subtle heart
of a greening industrial waste

water full of broken instruments
and scraps of torn paper
classifying a history of doubt

a few logs and bits of shattered machinery
a moment of delicate transition
where deception is second nature

the possibility of extreme revelation
among the nostalgic smells
of an abandoned railway station

a coffee stain and a pair of glasses
a shelf of persuasive spines
on mildewed books

a site of decayed meaning
an outlived revolution
among discarded cigarette cards

depicting cricketing greats
fine species of butterfly and moth
and forgotten venerable trees

we never mention our gods
among those who propagandise others
yet every morning the trucks collect the bodies

all deviations are corruptions of the text
we infer from experience
a subjective sequence of events

as multiple drafts of narrative fragments
coexist and coalesce turning
perception imperceptibly to memory

the grant of identity papers
is a great event conferring
the illusion of rights and citizenship

so we came into this land of spies
where borrowed language shifts
and seasons migrate

the days are no longer lost
what the memory has preserved
is never what happened

when the statue weeps it weeps blood
we seek the comfort of strangeness
a familiar landmark obscured by fog

with our end the world ends
someone has simply torn out
the last page

End of the Song

from which we deduce
barking of dogs in a demilitarised zone
an advance on our citizen rights

the chalky residue on my fingers
is from a phonograph recording
of my grandmother
thanking the delegates

documents of human evolution
and the skeletal remains
the sequence of river gravels and silts
surviving traces of the passage of ice

a shadowed place
of obscurely frightened souls

from which we deduce
ongoing expansion of the universe
lengthening of a particle wave
ad infinitum

a single cough resounding
in an empty auditorium

www.ingramcontent.com/pod-product-compliance
Lightning Source LLC
Chambersburg PA
CBHW022202080426
42734CB00006B/552